IT'S YOUR TIME

I0145014

IT'S YOUR TIME

A PROVEN TIME INVESTMENT PLAN TO ACHIEVE YOUR AMERICAN DREAM

RONALD LUCAS

PAGE PUBLISHING
4430 Lavon Drive, Suite 374-139
Garland, TX 75040

Cover design by Janet Long

ISBN: 978-0-9832212-1-0

Lucas, Ronald

It's Your Time/Ronald Lucas

Printed in USA

ACKNOWLEDGEMENTS

A special thanks to everyone who had a hand in helping make this book possible. I would like to especially thank and honor God for the wisdom and ability to write this book and the privilege to share these truths with the entire world. I would also like to thank my wife, Sylvia. It was through her love, passion and dedication for writing that my fire was kindled to write this book. To my children, Jahmal, Cecelia, Joshua and Joseph, thanks for being a driving force behind completing this book to leave an inheritance and a legacy for generations to come.

I also want to thank my mother, Cecelia Mae Jean Lucas, who planted and watered the seed to my understanding the value and principles of time. My father, Lenton Robert Lucas, gave me great advice that will last a lifetime. I would also like to thank the entire staff at Page Publishing, my editor Anita Robeson, Janet Long for page layout and cover design and David Brannon for photography. Last, but certainly not least, I would like to thank everyone who will read, learn and implement the principles in this book, plus share this information to help anyone who's seeking to achieve their American Dream.

Ecclesiastics 3:1: "To everything there is a season, and a time to every purpose under the heaven."

"IT'S YOUR TIME"

TABLE OF CONTENTS

ARE YOU AN AVERAGE AMERICAN?

- **The Average American worker hates his or her job.** 71% of Americans hate their jobs and are more likely to suffer from heart disease. Job dissatisfaction can also have negative impacts on children and marriages. *(Gallup Poll)*

- **The Average American lives for the next pay check.** The majority of Americans, 70%, live paycheck to paycheck with an average income of $43,000 a year, $3,800 in savings and $2,200 in credit card debt. *(Wall Street Journal)*

- **The Average American's medical problems are mainly stress-related.** 80% of medical expenses are stress-related and cost the nation $300 billion a year in medical bills and lost productivity. *(American Institute of Stress)*

- **The Average American is overweight.** More Americans than ever—66%—are clinically overweight, and 33% are obese (severely overweight). *(National Institutes of Health)*

- **The Average American is unable to balance work and life.** Many American workers (60-69%) don't have enough time for themselves, their marriage or their family. *(Workplace Flexibility in the United States)*

- **The Average American spends lots of free time watching TV.** Average Americans spend 33 hours per week viewing TV and 24 hours per month on social media. (Nielsen Ratings and Bureau of Labor Statistics)

- **The Average American may never achieve the American Dream.** 66% of Americans say the American Dream is becoming harder to achieve, especially for young families, mainly due to financial insecurity and poor-quality public education. (National League of Cities)

If you see yourself on this list, ***It's Your Time*** to

STOP STOP BEING AN AVERAGE AMERICAN

Sadly, the majority of Americans are not living the American Dream —they are living the American Nightmare!

What is the American Dream?

The American Dream represents limitless possibilities for success in life. To arrive there, you must plan, work and, ultimately, believe in your talents, abilities, gifts and skills. In this land of opportunity, your American Dream is your choice; it's your key to having a successful life.

The American Dream is attainable regardless of social or economic class, race, religion and/or ethnicity. More than 72% of Americans still believe people can start out poor and have the opportunity to get rich regardless of their initial circumstances. *(CBS News/New York Times)*

The American Dream is still attainable.

"Living the Dream" has nothing to do with current economic conditions or government policies. The traditional American Dream is based on the belief that hardworking citizens can better themselves, pay their monthly bills without worry, give their children a start to an even better life and still save enough to live comfortably after they retire. Unfortunately, the Average American makes the following basic mistakes when pursuing his or her dreams.

Basic mistakes when pursuing your dreams:

1. NOT UNDERSTANDING THE VALUE OF TIME.
2. NOT KNOWING HOW TIME WORKS.
3. WASTING TOO MUCH TIME.
4. NO VISION, DREAM OR GOALS.
5. NOT UNDERSTANDING THE DIFFERENCE BETWEEN SPENDING TIME AND INVESTING TIME.
6. NO TIME-INVESTMENT PLAN.

The goal of this book is to teach you how to apply the principles of time so you can achieve your American Dream.

It's Your Time provides you with a 30-day, step-by-step plan that teaches you how to invest your time to maximize your success in life and accomplish your dreams.

The American Dream isn't just for a select few; it's for anyone willing to invest the time. Life has provided everyone the same amount of time every day: 24 hours. That's it. No matter a person's social, economic or educational status, we all get the same amount of time.

The next step in the process is to understand and realize *It's Your Time*.

Time is our most important resource.

Some people say money is the most important resource on the planet, but I disagree. You can make more money, but no one can make more time.

Everyone gets 24 hours a day.

By understanding the value of time, learning how time works and establishing a time-investment plan, you can maximize your time on Earth and reach your God-given ability.

MY OWN STORY
AND HOW YOU CAN ACHIEVE
YOUR AMERICAN DREAM

My first encounters with the importance and value of time came from my mother when I was growing up in the inner-city projects of Chicago. She was a stickler about time. She believed your word was your bond, which meant if you said you would be somewhere at a particular time, you always kept your promise.

We grew up poor but didn't know it at the time. We never owned a house or a family car, and the only vacation we went on was to a relative's for a holiday. My mother was a single parent with six kids and only a partial high-school education, but she understood the value of time.

Over the past 30 years I have developed a time-investment plan that has afforded me the opportunity to graduate high school, attend college and work for some of the best companies in corporate America, including IBM, Caterpillar, Dennison MFG, Southwestern Bell, Fujitsu Networks Communications, White Rock Networks and Cisco Systems.

My American Dream was to be an engineer and business

owner. Despite coming from a humble beginning in Chicago, I've been able to climb the corporate ranks as an engineer, sales manager, sales director and sales vice president, all while generating six-figure salaries. Additionally, I've been able to invest my time to succeed as an insurance agent, Realtor, financial consultant, minister, youth director, entrepreneur, speaker, author and business consultant.

The American Dream is still available.

It's Your Time is a proven, step-by-step time-investment plan that over a 30-day period teaches you the principles that will allow you to maximize your success by investing your time wisely. *It's Your Time* to achieve your American Dream!

Invest 30 days to learn how to maximize your success in life.

Utilizing the principles and systems that I detail in this book, I was able to successfully navigate the maze of corporate America and my personal life. By utilizing the same time-investment principles, you too will be able to make more money by learning how to invest your time to maximize your success.

It's Your Time highlights the daily development system I used to plan, prepare and position myself for opportunities that propelled me to new levels of success in all aspects of life. The general principal is: Time operates like money and needs to be invested in proper areas to get a high rate of return.

Time operates like money.

Time is so valuable and precious that we must learn as soon as possible how to properly invest our time in order to reach our maximum potential. Stop wasting your time in all the wrong places, and invest your remaining time to learn the key principles by which time operates. This book will help you understand the value of time and finally discover the time-investment principles that will guide you to your success by maximizing your time every day.

My goal is to empower you and others to maximize your time on Earth in order to reach your full God-given ability, thereby achieving your American Dream.

Ronald Lucas

Ronald Lucas, T.I.M.E.

NOTES

CAN YOU INVEST YOUR TIME TO LIVE YOUR DREAM?

Over the years, time-management experts have presented countless complicated systems, programs and plans on how to manage and spend time—all with the goal of selling Americans high cost, low quality products and services. The simple truth is that time operates like money: In order to maximize your success in life, you must learn how to invest your time.

The simple truth is time operates like money.

You don't have to be a rocket scientist to understand how to invest time. People of average intelligence, like you and me, can do it if given the simple facts: Investing your time in the proper areas will increase your productivity, generate more income, motivate you, reduce stress, improve your health and help you to achieve your American Dream.

What you need is a Time Investment Plan!

First, I want to assure you that investing your time to maximize your future success is as simple as counting from one to five. If you can count to five, then you will be able to successfully utilize this proven Time Investment Plan.

Planning is the first step to taking control of your time. If you don't have a plan, you are planning to fail. If you have a plan and don't use it, you are wasting your time. Don't waste your time—follow this simple plan to achieve your dreams.

Some people say, "I don't have a dream." Then set a goal or get a picture of what you want and create a vision.

Time Investment Plan is as simple as counting from one to five.

I started using this plan in high school, so it had to be simple. Remember, the only requirement to utilizing this plan is the ability to count from one to five. There are seven basic time-investment principles outlined in this book. Each principle is a basic building block for the next principle, so make sure you follow the order of the book. The time-investment principles in this book are meant to guide you to a higher understanding of how time works and how to utilize the principles to invest your time to maximize your return on investment.

My plan has 7 basic principles:

1. Be responsible for your time.
2. Stop wasting your time.
3. Start investing your time.
4. Prioritize your time.
5. Balance your time.
6. Budget your time.
7. Establish your time.

PRINCIPLE #1
BE RESPONSIBLE FOR YOUR TIME

Time is defined as a limited period or interval between two events. Time is the beginning of the existence of our universe. Typically the two most important dates in a person's life are the time he/she was born and the time he/she dies. No matter what separates us—race, religion, finances, culture—everyone gets the same amount of time each day: 24 hours.

Everyone gets 24 hours per day.

Every day when you awake, thoughts begin to occupy your mind and fight for your time: what projects need to be completed, meetings attended, promises kept. All of a sudden you get overwhelmed, stressed and depressed—all before you get out of bed! Well I have some good news for you: Ultimately, you are personally responsible for your time. You have a choice, ***It's Your Time***.

Time is the most valuable resource on the planet. Many people say money is their most valuable resource, but I always tell them, "You can always make more money, but you can never make more time." You can count how much money you have in the bank and other investments, but you can't count how much time you have left on Earth. We need to learn to value our time. We don't get any more time, and we don't know how much we have left, so value time every day.

We need to value our time.

Circumstances can greatly impact our lives, but the Average American has the opportunity every day to choose what to do with his or her time. *It's Your Time*, and you have the right to determine how you are going to invest it in order to maximize your success in life. Most people talk about how to spend their time or manage their time, but you must learn how to invest your time if you are expecting a return on your investment. You can spend money or manage money all day, but you invest your money when you are expecting a profit. You must accept responsibility for your time and learn how to invest it to maximize your return. Everyone has 24 hours of time in a day; you are responsible for your time.

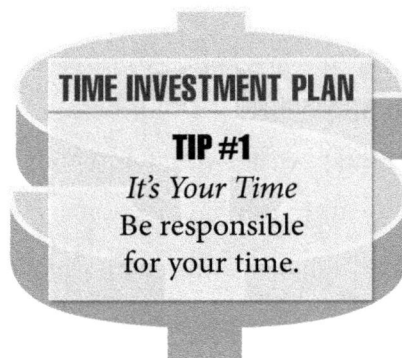

TIME INVESTMENT PLAN

TIP #1
It's Your Time
Be responsible
for your time.

It's Your Time to make a personal commitment to be responsible for your time.

PRINCIPLE #2
STOP WASTING YOUR TIME

Americans work more than anyone in the industrialized world. We work more than the English, more than the French, way more than the Germans or Norwegians. We even work more than the Japanese. Additionally, Americans take less vacation, work longer days and retire later. (ABC News, May 2012). Since Americans are hardworking people and we spend our time working, how come so many of us aren't "living the American Dream"?

Americans work more than anyone in the world.

As children we dreamed about being a doctor, lawyer, engineer, police officer, professional athlete, actor, singer or firefighter. We dreamed of being rich and owning a huge home with several new cars. The sky was the limit. We believed we could be whatever we wanted to be! So what happened? Where did our dreams go? Who or what took them away from us? The answer is that no one took away our dreams—we just lost track of time.

Americans have lost track of time.

Many people are working harder, but they don't understand there are certain principles of time that need to be followed to reach success. Since everyone gets the same amount of time in a day, how come some people accomplish so much more in their lifetime than others?

According to a recent survey conducted by the U.S. Bureau of

Labor Statistics and the Nielsen Ratings, here's how the average American spends his or her time:

How Americans Use Time

Activities	Hrs/Day
TV	4
Sleep	7
Video/Games	2
Texting	1
Internet	1
**Work/School	8
Miscellaneous	1
Total	24

** Bureau of Labor Statistics

Let's take a look at the time spent watching TV. If the average American spent four hours a day watching TV, by the time he or she reaches 65 years of age, that person would have spent approximately 10 years watching TV.

Four hours of TV a day waste 10 years of your life.

Many Americans spend considerably more than four hours a day watching TV programs and shows, especial with the invention of DVRs, Video on Demand, Internet TV, YouTube videos, and movies on smartphones. Do you watch more TV than the Average American? How much?

TV Viewing by Hours

Activities	Hrs/Day	Hrs/Week	Years Spent
TV	3	21	8
TV	5	35	13
TV	7	49	18
TV	9	63	23

If you spend an average of seven hours every day watching TV or some other form of video media, after 65 years you would have spent 18 years watching media. This is equivalent to putting a newborn in front of a TV for 18 years, then sending him or her to kindergarten. Not a pretty picture.

Don't get me wrong, I like to watch TV just as much as the next person, but I only have so much time remaining on Earth, and I am ultimately responsible for how I invest my time.

Seven hours of TV a day wastes 18 years of your life.

I find these statistics quite alarming. I can't imagine spending that much time in front of the TV and wasting 18 years of my life. The Average American doesn't look at how much time he or she wastes over a lifetime, just the time he/she spent today.

To maximize your success in life, you need to look at how you invest your time throughout your life. I don't want to waste much of my time on activities that don't benefit me or provide a return on my time investments. Time operates like money: If you invest it over a period of time in areas that are yielding a high return, your investments will grow.

Invest your time in high yield areas.

The average American spends 24 hours a month on social media sites. In the U.S. alone, a collective 12 billion hours are spent each day on social media networks. The average American is interrupted every 10 minutes by social media, including during work hours. Social media interruptions cost the U.S. economy $650 billion a year.

Social media interruptions cost the U.S. $650 billion a year.

Our time is so precious and valuable that every person, business and organization in the world is trying to produce and develop programs, products and ideas that will occupy our time. I am not saying you can't enjoy the benefits of technological advancements, but you only get so much time on this Earth.

The Bible says, "To everything there is a season, and a time to every purpose under the heaven." If there is a time for everything, then there's a time limit for everything. We must learn to limit our time in certain areas in order to maximize our opportunities in the areas that will yield a greater return on our time investments.

We must learn to limit our time in certain areas.

So many people go through their life trying to figure out why only a few people prosper and so many others live an average life. Thousands of books have been written about the secrets to becoming rich and famous. Numerous magazine stories and television, radio and online programs feature individuals coming from other countries to America to get rich. And yet, the average American born on U.S.

soil can't seem to discover the secrets to achieving his or her dreams.

Stop blaming others for your lack of success.

Many times we take the easy way out by blaming our lack of success on other people, our family, our education, our circumstances, our society, our government and our economy. We even blame it on God. But the real reason we lack the success we seek is based on how we invest our time. *It's Your Time*, so stop wasting it.

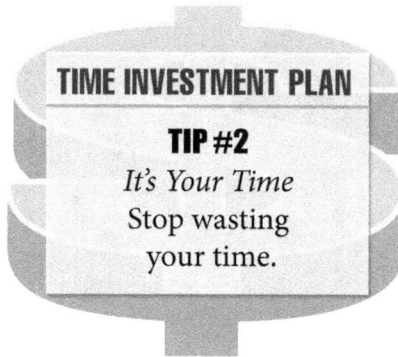

TIME INVESTMENT PLAN

TIP #2
It's Your Time
Stop wasting
your time.

NOTES

PRINCIPLE #3
START INVESTING YOUR TIME

Time often operates like money. First, people normally invest money with the understanding and expectation that they will get their money back along with a profit or a return on their investment. To maximize your life opportunity, time must also be invested in areas that are yielding a profitable return.

Time must be invested in areas that yield a profit.

Second, money must be budgeted. A budget tells your money where to go before you get it, or you might spend more than you had anticipated. Time works in a similar way. You need to create a time budget or list (things to do, honey do's, tasks, action items, etc.) to tell your time where to go before you get it. This is the basis for your Time Investment Plan—you must tell your time where to go before you get your next 24 hours' worth of time.

Tell your time where to go before you get it.

Successful people develop the habit of writing down exactly how they plan to invest their time once they get it. Before they go to bed, they invest some time to write down a list of things they need to do if they get another 24 hours' worth of time. When they get up in the morning the first thing they do is take out their list and begin working on their most important tasks. Planning your day ahead of time gives you a clear picture of what needs to be done to bring you closer to your dream, goal or vision.

Determine how to invest your time before you get it.

One of the main reasons the Average American never achieves his or her goals is because more than 80% of Americans don't have any goals. Just 16% of Americans have goals but don't write them down, fewer than 4% write down their goals and fewer than 1% review their goals on an ongoing basis. The study, by Professor Emeritus Dave Kohl at Virginia Tech, concluded that people who regularly write down their goals earn nine times as much income over their lifetime as people who don't.

People who write down their goals
earn nine times more money.

By writing down your goals you are automatically ahead of 96% of the population in terms of the potential to become financially successful. Every morning when you awake, all the cares of the day begin to occupy your thoughts. Your concerns, things you need to do, action items, meetings, calls, etc., all began to fight for your immediate attention and time. The average American has so many things on his or her agenda that just waking up becomes stressful and depressing. The key to this situation is to treat your time like you treat your money. Money needs to be budgeted before you get it, and time needs to be invested before you get it. You need to invest your time the night prior to receiving your next 24 hours.

Invest your time the night before you get it.

Every night before you go to bed take out a clean sheet of paper and invest approximately 10 to 15 minutes to write down the Top 5 goals, tasks or items you need to complete, assuming you get another 24 hours deposited into your life account.

Here are a couple of questions that will help stimulate you to create a list and identify your five most important items. What are my primary goals? What do I need to do to accomplish my goals? Do I have any honey do's? Have I made any promises or commitments to my children? Do I have any work or business deadlines? Whom do I need to call? What do I need to do for myself?

After you finish writing your list of things that need to be done, review the list and highlight the Top 5 items you need to complete the next day. First thing the next morning, take out your list and begin to work on completing those Top 5 items you highlighted the night before.

Invest your time in your Top 5 items.

The following diagram highlights an example of a Top 5 list.

Top 5 Model Diagram

	Top 5
	Meet with attorney
	Organize office
	Take deposit to bank
	Meet with customer
	Take mother to doctor

At this point, invest the next 10-15 minutes to think about all the items or tasks you need to complete tomorrow to move you closer to accomplishing your goals. After you complete the list, highlight the Top 5 items you must complete.

First thing the next morning, take out your list and begin to work on completing those Top 5 items. Continue this process for the next seven days. This step in the Time Investment Plan teaches you how to invest your time.

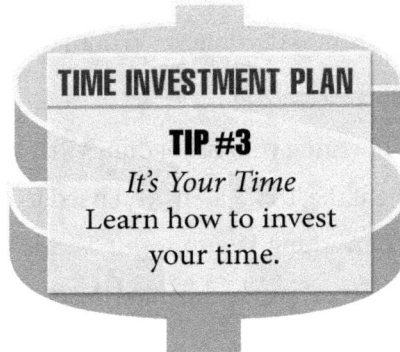

TIME INVESTMENT PLAN

TIP #3

It's Your Time
Learn how to invest
your time.

PRINCIPLE #4
PRIORITIZE YOUR TIME

During your most productive years life can become complicated, especially when you are juggling so many balls in the air. We have so many things we need to do for ourselves, our families, our jobs or businesses, our social organizations, our religious affiliations. For most people life can get so hectic and demanding that they don't know where to begin.

Most people don't know where to begin.

One of life's biggest challenges is to determine what to do with our time and the right time to do those things. We only have 24 hours in a day, and we need to invest our time every day to reach our maximum life potential. The areas we choose to invest our time in today will determine our success tomorrow and beyond. Our ability to identify the correct task and its priority is another key to a successful life.

Identify the correct task and right priority.

I had always prided myself on the ability to complete tasks in a timely fashion, but learning to set priorities revolutionized my way of thinking about investing my time. There is always an abundance of options for things you can be doing with your time, but what is the right thing to do that will bring you closer to your dreams, goals or vision?

When you take the time to write down your dreams, goals or vision, you are signing a virtual contract with yourself that says you are agreeing to do whatever is required to accomplish those goals. Once the contract is signed and executed, you are acknowledging to yourself that these goals are your priority and the most important areas in which to invest your time.

Write down your dreams, goals or vision for your life.

At this point, invest the next 10-15 minutes to think about what is the most important short-term goal you want to accomplish in your life. For the sake of this process think of something you can accomplish within the next seven days.

Every night before you go to bed write down the Top 5 tasks you need to complete the next day, assuming you get another 24 hours' worth of time. Next, alongside your Top 5 tasks indicate the order of importance by putting a priority number from 1–5 next to each item. This will help you identify which item or task to start working on when you get up the next day.

Start with high priority items first.

By starting with the high priority items, you are maximizing your time to accomplish your goals. This diagram shows the Top 5 model using priority numbers to highlight which item to start first.

Top 5 Model With Priority

Priority	Top 5
4	Meet with attorney
5	Organize office
2	Take deposit to bank
3	Meet with customer
1	Take mother to doctor

(Example only)

Again, you can see that time operates like money. When you create a budget you identify the priority areas—mortgage or rent, lights, gas, telephone, transportation, etc.—in which to allocate your money so you can maintain a certain quality of life. Time operates similarly, since when you create your Top 5 list, you identify the priority areas in which to invest your time in order to attain your goals.

Identify the priority areas in which to invest your time.

One of the most amazing things I noticed from this process is that when you take care of the high priority items first, you have more time to take care of everything else. I know there's no such thing as making more time, but you get a sense of peace and progress from completing the high priority items, and that, in turn, makes you feel like you can accomplish more. But most important, you invested your time to accomplish the priority items that will give you a greater return on your time.

20% of your efforts produce 80% of the results.

The 80/20 rule of time management teaches that approximately 20% of your efforts produce 80% of the results. To look at this another way, 20% of the things you do generate 80% of your revenues. Learning to recognize and then focus on that 20% is the key to making the most effective use of your time. There are many good things you can be doing with your time, but to maximize the effective use of your time you must prioritize.

Always keep first things first.

During this process, and on your journey to accomplishing your American Dream, you will run into opposition. Encountering opposition is a part of life's process. But meeting opposition doesn't necessary mean you have to quit or give up on your dream or goal.

Many people fall apart when their goals or plans meet opposition. Your dreams and goals will never be accomplished unless you are willing to pay the price. The cost of a dream might be paid many times during the time it takes to accomplish and maintain your goal. The initial cost of your dream will require you to make personal and painful sacrifices. Sometimes you will have to deny yourself some of life's most treasured pastimes and pleasures, like watching TV or playing video games or a round of golf. You might even have to walk away from some attractive options and valued relationships because they are pulling you in the opposite direction of your dream, goal or vision.

Opposition is a part of the journey to the dream.

Sometimes when you are driving a car, you run into an unexpected detour on your way to your final destination. You must be like a GPS system and recalculate, reroute or go around the opposition in order to reach your desired destination. You might need to go another route, but your destination remains the same. Life can provide many roadblocks and detours along the highway to your dream, but you must overcome these obstacles by discovering an alternate path.

On occasion you encounter a closed door to your dream.

At certain times the opposition you encounter is a closed door. The goal or dream you are pursuing may no longer be available or relevant. For example, let's say your dream is to be a professional basketball player. During the course of the journey you encounter an injury that prohibits you from playing basketball. In a situation like this, the sooner you realize the opportunity is no longer available, the better. You will need to establish a new goal, dream or vision for your life. Life is a discovery process. You never know which dream or goal will actually provide you with the maximum success you desire. You only have so much time on Earth to discover your purpose and live your dream; the sooner you start working on achieving your dreams, goals and plans, the more you can accomplish. Remember, *It's Your Time.*

You only have so much time on Earth to live your dream.

During the initial seven days, you developed the habit of writing down the Top 5 items that needed to be completed. During the next seven days, you will develop the habit of writing down the Top 5 items you need to complete along with the order of priority. Remember: Start with first things first.

Every night before you go to bed, invest 10-15 minutes to write down your Top 5 list with the priority number for each item. First thing in the morning, start working on the task with the highest priority. Once you complete the highest priority item, start on the task with the next highest priority. Continue this process until all items have been completed. Follow this process for the next seven days.

TIME INVESTMENT PLAN

TIP #4
It's Your Time
Choose the correct priority; first things first.

PRINCIPLE #5
BALANCING YOUR TIME

At this point, you've been writing down your Top 5 list every day for the past 14 days and writing down your prioritized Top 5 list for the past seven days. If you have completed this process, you will notice an immediate increase in your productivity simply because you have been investing your time every night to think about and create a list of what you were going to accomplish with your time.

Productivity measures accomplishment toward your dream.

Productivity is a measure of how much you accomplish toward your dream. It's far better to prioritize how you will invest your time; you'll achieve more with your time and resources. The Time Investment Plan will increase your productivity and allow you more time to do extra things. Just by writing down your Top 5 list and prioritizing your tasks, you are already positioned to be more successful than 96% of Americans.

Life would be so much easier if we only had five things to do every day, but the truth is our lives are much more complicated than just five items. Here again, time operates like money. You don't want to put all your money investments in one basket, and you need to make sure you don't invest all your time in one area.

Balance your time investments in different areas.

Your time needs to be invested into different areas to make sure you balance your time to maximize our success. Your Time Investment Plan identifies four major categories in which to invest your time in order to keep the foundation of your life in balance: God, Self, Home/Family, Work/Business.

Invest your time in the four categories of time.

Investing time in these four areas provides a solid foundation on which to lay the roof of your American Dream. We will examine each of these four walls in detail so you can understand how to invest in each area in order to maximize your time investments.

Invest time in God.

The American Dream was built on America's trust and dependency on God. We even put "In God We Trust" on the back of our currency to highlight the importance of investing time with God. The overwhelming majority of Americans believe in God: According to a recent survey, 92% of Americans believe in God, and more than half of Americans pray at least once a day. (Pew Forum on Religion and Public Life)

92% of Americans believe in God.

God is one of the major categories in which we need to invest our time. Many people believe that by attending church they are investing in God, but I don't believe this is the case. I believe people need to make a separation between God and church. God is the Supreme Being and Creator of the entire world, and we need to invest time to get to know Him through prayer, study, fasting, meditation, devotion and service. Church is typically a building where people of like faith gather for fellowship and worship.

Many people believe that going to church just once a month satisfies the time investment in getting to know God, but every believer needs to invest time to develop a personal relationship with God. Just over 90% of Americans pray every day, and in fact half pray several times a day. (*Washington Times*) But according to the Barna Survey, the average Christian invests only one minute a day in prayer and the average pastor invests only five minutes a day in prayer.

The Average American prays a total of one minute a day.

By the way, those numbers also include when we pray over our food. In order to maintain a healthy, close relationship with anyone, especially the God we are trusting with our entire lifetime, you will need to invest more than just one minute a day in prayer. I would recommend initially investing a minimum of 15 minutes a day in prayer.

Invest 15 minutes a day to prayer.

The Average American **reads** or studies his or her Bible 52 minutes a week, or approximately 7.5 minutes a day. How well would you know your job if you only invested seven minutes a day to reading to learn about the company's products and services? I would gather you wouldn't be very knowledgeable about your company. I would recommend investing 15 minutes a day reading your Bible.

Invest 15 minutes each day to reading your Bible.

Fasting is the practice of abstaining from food for a set purpose and a set period of time in order to pray as an act of faith unto your God. For example, the normal practice of fasting would involve abstaining from food for a full day. This would start first thing in the morning and continue until the following morning, when you would eat again and break the fast.

Fast for at least one meal once a week.

Of course you might decide to miss just one or two meals in a day in order to pray and fast. Some people fast for three days or a week. A normal fast would be abstinence from food but not water. It is important to drink water during a fast. It also is important to be alone with God in prayer. There is no point in choosing a day that is busy or full of distractions or when a lot of people are around you. Choose a day when you can be quiet and alone with God. I recommend fasting one meal at least once a week.

Meditation is the mental discipline of investing time to relax the mind into a deeper state of self-awareness. Mediation allows you to focus and quiet your thoughts and listen to your self-awareness. Meditation helps you to become aware of your inner thoughts to identify upcoming tasks and action items.

Devotion is taking the time to meditate on a particular word, phrase, verse or story in the Bible. There are many daily-devotion books available at book stores that highlight a particular principle you can read in about three minutes. You might be saying, this is just too much time to invest in just one category, but when we recap you can see this entire category only requires a total time investment of one hour of time per day for God.

Invest one hour of time a day with God.

The Average American spends three-four hours a day watching TV. Americans can spend up to eight-12 hours a day watching TV, depending on the sport and season. Most of the time, we distance ourselves from God unconsciously; we become preoccupied, self-centered or over-committed, and before you know it, prayer is limited to grace over meals, Bible reading to the pastor's sermon text and worship to Sunday morning messages. The American Dream was built on the promise that God will bless America. You must make it a goal to close the gap between you and God! In order to make more money, you will need to invest time into building a stronger relationship with your core belief system and faith in God. The following model illustrates this.

Top 5 God Category Model

	Top 5
Priority	GOD
4	Fast – Dinner (Wed.)
5	Meditate – 15 minutes
2	Read Bible – 15 minutes
3	Devotion – 5 minutes
1	Prayer – 15 minutes

(Example only)

Every night before you go to bed invest time to think about and identify the Top 5 items or tasks you need to do for God. Write down the most important five that come to mind and number them according to priority. Fasting can be done on any day of the week during any meal of the day, but I would recommend standardizing it on a particular day of the week for consistency and commitment.

Invest time in Self.

Many people teach that you should take care of your home or family before you take care of yourself, but I disagree. I believe in the airplane model: "Please put on your oxygen mask before assisting your children or someone else in your area." What good would it be to achieve your financial American Dream only to be in bad health and spend all your hard-earned resources on doctors and medicines? This would be the American Nightmare. When we are putting together our Time Investment Plan for our Self category, we should consider investing time in both our physical health (exercise, eating) and mental health (reading, relaxing).

Invest time in your physical health.

Most Americans exercise about two hours each week or 17 minutes a day. Health experts at Penn State, the University of Maryland and the U.S. Centers for Disease Control and Prevention recommend we exercise four hours a week for optimal health. That could include about 2.5 hours of moderate exercise and about an hour-and-a-half of vigorous activity, such as running and muscle strengthening. According to a professor emeritus of recreation, park and tourism management at Penn State, "The United States is the fattest country in the world. The amount of exercise Americans get has become a major concern."

Invest 35 minutes a day in exercising.

When health in the United States is compared to health in other countries, the picture is disappointing. In an often-cited report from 2000, the World Health Organization ranked the U.S. health-care system 37th in the world, despite the fact that per-capita health-care spending here continues to lead the world. Physical inactivity is a major contributor to disease worldwide and is the fourth leading risk factor for global mortality. With roughly a third of the world's population inactive, physical inactivity is responsible for an estimated 6-10% of non-communicable diseases, including heart disease, Type 2 diabetes, breast cancer and colon cancer.

In U.S., 40% of the population is physically inactive.

Overall, inactivity is responsible for 9% of premature deaths—5.3 million deaths in 2008 alone. In the U.S., 40% of the population is physically inactive, which is higher than both Canada at 34% and Mexico at 38%. It is estimated that eliminating physical inactivity in the U.S. could add nearly a year to life expectancy and dramatically reduce the burden of chronic diseases.

Obesity is another major contributor to disease. North America has 34% of the world's biomass due to obesity, yet it only makes up 6% of the world's population. Asia, on the other hand, has 61% of the world's population yet only 13% of its biomass due to obesity. While the U.S. is only one of several countries that make up North America, it is the only North American nation to rank in the heaviest 10. Despite the highest per-capita spending on health care, the U.S. doesn't fare well in most comparisons to other developed countries. The U.S. has some of the most state-of-the-art health-care facilities, yet behavioral factors such as physical inactivity, smoking and dietary choices result in poor performance. Many people join health clubs to help them stay committed, but 90% will stop going within the first 90 days.

90% of Americans who join health clubs quit within 90 days.

Another important part of the health equation is what we are eating and drinking. Have you noticed that restaurants that offer large portions have a lot of large customers? Portion size is one of the main indicators of Americans' overeating. Fifty years ago, portion sizes were smaller and relatively healthy. But as fast-food franchises began to increase in the 1960s and '70s, portion sizes grew quite a bit. The chains were eager to offer customers larger portions for a better "sense of value." It's important to also note that portion size as a key factor in weight gain and obesity has increased since the 1970s in both adults and children.

Another important statistic to keep in mind is that 54% of Americans will eat until their plate is clean. So as our portion sizes have ballooned, so have our appetites. Between 1977 and 1996, portion sizes and energy intake increased for almost all key foods.

The good news is that we know what a properly portioned meal should look like. First, use a smaller plate; something around 7-9 inches is perfect. If your plate is larger than that, you'll add more food to make it appear full and most likely will eat it all. Also, what is on your plate should be portioned correctly.

Eat smaller portions of food.

If, for instance, you are having a plate of grilled chicken, broccoli and mashed potatoes, half of your plate should be broccoli, one-fourth chicken and one-fourth mashed potatoes. If you are concerned about your portion or plate size, divide your plate in half. Half should be filled with fruits and vegetables and the other half equal parts of protein and starch.

The Average American is clinically overweight.

Today, more Americans than ever—66%, according to the

National Institutes of Health—are clinically overweight, while one in three is obese (severely overweight). In fact, figures released by the Centers for Disease Control and Prevention show that the nation's obesity rose 6% between 1998 and 1999 alone. The average weight for a 10-year-old boy in 1963 was 74.2 pounds; by 2002, the average weight was nearly 85 pounds. The average weight for a 10-year-old girl in 1963 was 77.4 pounds; by 2002, the average weight was nearly 88 pounds. Over the past three decades, the childhood obesity rate has more than doubled for preschool children aged 2 to 5 years and adolescents aged 12 to 19 years, and more than tripled for children aged 6 to 11 years. At present, approximately 9 million children over 6 years of age are considered obese and 15 percent are considered at risk of becoming overweight.

9 million children over age 6 are obese.

Unfortunately, because Americans have increased their portions, their daily calorie intake has also increased. That is largely due to the growth in sweets, the mass consumption of soft drinks and the prevalence of alcohol. Sweets, desserts, soft drinks and alcoholic beverages account for nearly 25 percent of all calories consumed by Americans. Healthy fruits and vegetables make up only 10% of caloric intake in the U.S. diet.

Invest less time in eating sweets and soft drinks.

In the last 20 years, we have really buttoned down on heart disease and strokes and their connection to high sodium intake. The definitive studies, the DASH study and the DASH sodium study, only came out in the 1990s and were the first to definitively link the two. The news is not good, however, as our consumption of processed foods, which are high in sodium, has continued to rise. American adults ingest nearly 4,000 mg of sodium daily on average, far exceeding current recommendations.

Eat less salt per day.

The Department of Health and Human Services and the World Health Organization, along with other organizations, support a daily sodium intake of no more than 2,400 mg. Adults who are middle-aged, elderly, already have hypertension or pre-hypertension, or have a family history of hypertension should consume less than 1,500 mg. The main culprit is salt in processed and restaurant foods. The good news is that it is easy to lower your sodium intake. In this economy, people are beginning to cook at home more and more, something that is so important to maintaining a healthy diet. By preparing your meals and your family's, you control the salt in your food.

There are basically four kinds of fats: saturated, monounsaturated, polyunsaturated and trans. Lately, trans fats have become such a hot topic that they have been eliminated from fast-food chains and most restaurants. We know that saturated and trans fats are bad for us, but not too long ago, experts believed that eating more cholesterol caused cholesterol to accumulate in the bloodstream and on artery walls. That meant foods high in cholesterol but otherwise heart-healthy, like eggs or shrimp, were considered just as taboo as a stick of butter. Thankfully, research has matured in recent years and scientific opinion has changed. We now know that cholesterol levels are largely influenced by the kind of fat we eat. Two helpers are monounsaturated fats (in olives, avocados, and olive and canola oils) and polyunsaturated fats (found in vegetable oils, soybeans, fish, shellfish, and seeds). Nuts are rich sources of both. We know that these fats are important to a heart-healthy diet, and they add tons of flavor and variety to everyday eating. If you want to cut down on your fat intake, avoid saturated fats such as butter or deeply fried foods. Stick to salmon, olive oil, nuts and all-natural peanut butter.

Reduce fat in your diet.

The Mediterranean diet typical of traditional Italian and Greek cooking has been found to be one of the healthiest eating patterns in the world. This diet consists mainly of fruits and veggies, beans and nuts, whole grains, fish, olive oil, small amounts of dairy and meat, and red wine. Also, traditional Japanese cooking, with fresh fish and vegetables at every meal, is known to be healthful. In recent years, many regions of the world have started to adopt a more American eating pattern of fast foods, processed foods and larger portions. As a result, countries in Asia, notably China, and even Europe, such as the United Kingdom and France, are experiencing a rise in obesity.

The Average American doesn't read self-help books.

Another area in which we need to invest time is self-help and

personal-development books or courses. This involves reading books and studying new material to keep the brain functioning and to create new money-making opportunities, growth and career advancement. I heard a great saying that gives validity to this point: "If you want to get ahead, put something in your head."

We are living in the information age–people pay you for what you know, and you pay for what you don't know! One in four adults, or 25%, read no books at all in the past year, according to an Associated Press poll. Of those who did read, women and older people were the most avid, and religious works and popular fiction were the top choices.

If you want to get ahead, put something in your head.

People who read invested 18 minutes a day in leisure reading that included books, magazines, computer articles, e-books and cellphones. (U.S. Bureau of Labor Statistics) The Pew Research Center has unveiled its stats on the United States' reading habits in 2012, revealing that 75% of Americans aged 16 and above read at least one book this year. What the survey doesn't mention is that according to reports, only 60% of these readers got past the first chapter.

Based on these surveys, it's safe to say the majority of Americans don't read self-help books. Too bad, because avid readers often make more money in America. According to an article by Mike Myatt, chief strategy officer at N2growth, "All great leaders have one thing in common: They read voraciously." The average CEO typically reads four-five books a month.

CEOs invest time every month to read four-five books.

Do the math: CEOs typically read four-five books a month, or 48-60 books a year. The average CEO pay for companies in the S&P 500 Index rose to $12.94 million in 2011. Overall, the average level of CEO pay in the S&P 500 Index increased 13.9 percent in 2011, following a 22.8 percent increase in CEO pay in 2010. According to Salary.com, the median expected salary for a typical chief executive officer in the United States is $732,744.

The Average CEO makes approximately $13 million per year.

2011 Average CEO Pay at S&P 500 Index Companies	
Salary	$1,091,182
Bonus	$268,110
Stock awards	$5,279,828
Option awards	$2,352,544
Non-equity incentive plan compensation	$2,382,529
Pension and deferred compensation earnings	$1,308,625
All other compensation	$252,657
TOTAL	$12,935,47

Based on these numbers, reading is one of the principle factors in generating more income in America. One of the reasons college can justify raising the cost of education is that people with a bachelor's degree make 84% more over a lifetime than high school graduates. On average, a person with a doctoral degree will earn

$3.3 million over a lifetime, compared to $2.3 million for a college graduate and $1.3 million for those with a high school diploma.

College graduates make 84% more over a lifetime.

People with less education in high-paying occupations can out-earn their counterparts with advanced degrees. But within the same industry, workers with more schooling usually land better paychecks. (Georgetown's Center on Education and the Workforce)

Invest one hour of time a day for yourself.

My point is that people who read or study independently make more money. Here's an example of how that would look.

Top 5 Self Category Model

	Top 5
Priority	Self
4	Relax – 25 minutes
5	Fun activity – 30 minutes
2	Eat – Mediterranean diet
3	Read – 30 minutes
1	Exercise – 35 minutes

(Example only)

Every night before you go to bed, invest time to identify the Top 5 items or tasks you need to do for God and for Self. Write down the top five items in each category and number them according to their priority.

Don't worry if you only have three items per category; in time, your number of items will increase. Understand that the difference between the person you currently are and the person you would like to become will largely be based upon your relationships and your reading habits. If you are looking for your American Dream or just to make more money, you need to learn how to invest your time in these two major investment areas.

Invest time in Home/Family.

The next category we need to invest time in is at home. Have a Time Investment Plan for your spouse, children, finances and physical-house responsibilities.

Marriage is part of the American Dream. The majority of people want to have a family. The American Dream family typically consists of husband, wife and several children. Everyone is looking to find his or her true love, someone to build a lifelong loving relationship with, to depend on when crisis comes along and to share joyful moments with. The wedding vows are a promise to love, honor, trust and serve your spouse in sickness and health, in adversity and prosperity, and to be true and loyal so long as you both shall live.

The American Dream is to find your true love.

The American Dream is to find your true love and live happily ever after, but more than 50% of marriages in the U.S. end in divorce. According to recent surveys, 95% of divorces are caused by lack of communication. The average working person invests less than two minutes per day in meaningful communication with his or her spouse or significant other.

Average American communicates two minutes with a spouse.

Divorce has a tremendous impact on children and adults and on society as a whole. According to the National Center of Health and Statistics:

- After a divorce, women experience a 45% drop in their standard of living.

- In 1996, children of divorce were 50% more likely than their counterparts from intact families to divorce.

- Fatherless homes account for 63% of youth suicides, 90% of homeless/runaway children, 85% of children with behavior problems, 71% of high school dropouts, 85% of youths in prison, and well over 50% of teen mothers.

Instead of the American Dream, divorce is creating an American Nightmare. You must invest time to make your marriage work.

Invest 15 minutes in meaningful communication with spouse.

Part of the American Dream is to have loving, healthy and disciplined children. As you can see from the previous statistics, divorce is devastating for the children. A study by the Center for Mental Health Services concluded that children whose fathers actively invested time in their school and social lives perform better on standardized testing, have higher levels of self-esteem and run a lower risk of experimenting with alcohol, drugs and other illegal activities.

Children with an active father in their life perform better.

People are living busier lives and spending more time at work, but parents need to find the time to invest in their children. Children learn about families from the time they spend in their own families. They learn about birth and caring for another person when a new baby comes home from the hospital. They learn about loss when a family member dies. They learn about marriage and relationships by watching their mothers and fathers interact. By living in a family, children learn to share, how to stand up for their rights and how to love another person.

Many parents can't seem to find the time to teach their children to read, write or ride a bike, but the Average American finds the time to invest 28 hours a week in watching television. We need to change our priorities and invest time with our children. Investing time in our children is valuable and important for the survival of the American Dream.

The Average American spends more time with TV than kids.

I have three children at home and know firsthand the difficulty of finding the time to invest in my children, especially after a full day at work of battling with customers, vendors, partners, internal deadlines and other exhausting projects. On top of that, people are working longer hours and spending less time in leisure activities.

For example, 40% of employees said their workload had increased in the past 12 months, causing stress and preventing them from investing more time in their family. In a recent Gallup Poll, 80% of workers said they feel stress on the job, impacting how they relate to their family. We must find the time to invest in our children; children are the future and our legacy in America. We must invest time in the next generation. The Bible says, "Train up a child in the way they should go and when they are old they will not depart."

We must invest time in training the next generation.

I don't believe anyone purposely makes plans for their children to drop out of school, go to prison, be on drugs or wind up in the alcohol rehab center, but if we can't find the time to invest in our children, the statistics speak for themselves. According to a study from Pennsylvania State University, the time teens spend with their fathers may have critical benefits. For example, the more time invested alone with their fathers, the higher their self-esteem; the more time with their dads in a group setting, the better their social skills.

Invest 15 minutes in meaningful communication with your children.

Over the past 20 years, working time on the job has increased by approximately 15% and our leisure time has decreased about 33%. Americans are working harder and relaxing less. We need to invest time to rejuvenate our minds and bodies. Without investing time for relaxation and leisure, life just becomes a 9-to-5 grind. I remember my mother saying, "Smell the roses before you die."

Invest 30 minutes a day in leisure and relaxation.

The Average American makes $43,000 a year, a total of about $1.7 million over 40 working years. If a person or family makes $100,000 a year, that equals $4 million over 40 working years. The majority of Americans are looking for the financial American Dream, but the truth is that the Average American has more than $2 million flowing through his/her hands during a lifetime.

The Average American generates more than $2 million in a lifetime.

An important fact I've learned during this life is that success isn't based on how much you make during your lifetime, it's based on how much you keep and invest to maximize your return on investment.

Let's use as an example a couple (starting at age 30) that made $48,000 a year and saved 15% ($7,200 per year or $600 per month) in a 401K at 12% growth. When they're 70 years old, they will have $7 million in the 401K. (Dave Ramsey)

$600 per month investment at 12% interest yields $7 million.

If that same couple fully funded a Roth IRA at $5,000 each per year ($833 per month at 12% growth), at age 70 they would have an additional $9.8 million – tax free!

$833 per month investment at 12% interest yields $9.8 million.

And finally, what if that same couple, debt free, does both? At age 70, they would have a combined total of $16.8 million.

But the reality about the Average American's finances is this:

- The Average American income is $43,000 per year.

- The Average American family has $3,800 in the bank.

- Average credit-card debt is $2,200.

- Nearly 70% of all Americans live from paycheck to paycheck. (*Wall Street Journal*)

- Approximately 2 million people file for bankruptcy each year. (American Bankruptcy Institute)

- The combined amount of personal debt held by Americans is $2 trillion.

- Conflict over money is the leading cause of divorce. (*Psychology Today*)

The American Dream is not based on what you make, it's based on what you keep and invest to maximize your return on your investment for future growth and opportunity.

Invest time to learn how to save and invest your money.

A marriage is a business partnership where the officers (husband and wife) and employees (children) need to meet to invest time to discuss the various areas of the family business, such as marriage, home, finances and children. I recommend having a family business meeting once a week for meaningful communication and to discuss the family plans, goals, events, food, needs and schedules that you'll need to invest time in during the upcoming week.

Invest time in a family meeting once a week.

Family meetings are necessary to bring the entire family together to discuss concerns and to make plans for the following week. During the family meeting you discuss financial matters, travel requirements, school fees or events, chore assignments, meal plans, important dates and weekly schedules. Here is an example of a Home/Family priority list.

Top 5 Home Category Model

	Top 5
Priority	Home
4	Confirm date night
5	Repair air conditioner
2	Clean garage
3	Pay bills
1	Household budget

(Example only)

Every night before you go to bed invest time to think and identify the Top 5 items or tasks you need to do for God, Self and Home. Write down the Top 5 items in each category that come to mind and number them according to their priority.

Don't worry if you only have three items per category; in time, your items will increase. If you are looking for your American Dream or just to make more money, then you need to learn how to invest your time in these three major investment areas.

Invest time in Work/Business.

The American Dream at work represents personal independence and self-reliance on one's talents, abilities, gifts and skills to support our existence. A hundred years ago only 5% of Americans worked for companies; today, 95% do.

95% of Americans work for companies.

During the Industrial Age, Americans traded independence for the security of a job. By the 1950s the American Dream was found in education. That was the path to management—the good life. Nationwide, only 24% of job openings in 2012 were available to people without at least some post-secondary education. A whopping 43% of job openings require a bachelor's degree or more. It's easy to see why, as of May 2012, unemployment among those with a high school diploma or less is 6 percentage points higher than among those with a bachelor's degree or more. (Brookings Institution) It's better to have a college degree and not need it than to need a college degree and not have it. It's time to get a traditional college education if you are planning to obtain a career in a traditional job.

24% of jobs are available to Americans without a college degree.

Americans work more than anyone in the industrialized world. We work more than the English, more than the French, way more than the Germans or Norwegians, even more than the Japanese. Additionally, Americans take less vacation, work longer days and retire later. (ABC News, May 2012)

71% of Americans hate their job.

Americans work more than anyone in the industrialized world, but 71% of Americans hate their job and are disengaged from their work. (Gallup Poll) Since 1979, 54 million Americans have been laid off!

What do Americans workers worry about? Some 30% are worried about losing their job, another 30% say they are worried their hours will be cut back and another 33% worry their wages will be reduced. An even larger number, 44%, worry their benefits will be reduced, making this the most prevalent job-related concern. The U.S. Bureau of Labor Statistics indicates that approximately 2 million employees in the private sector are fired every year, and it is estimated that about 10% of those, or at least 150,000 workers, are fired for no legitimate reason.

A new survey by Right Management, the consulting arm of the staffing group Manpower, finds that a whopping 84% of employees want to leave their job.

84% of Americans want to leave their job.

The stress of believing you could lose your job worsens satisfaction levels in other areas of life, such as God, Self and Home/Family.

The Average American receives more information via mail, email, social media and text on a daily basis than the average person alive in 1900 received in a lifetime. The inability of an individual to effectively organize, manage, process and balance this information in a timely manner creates stress. Stress-related illness costs the nation $300 billion a year in medical costs and lost productivity. (American Institute of Stress)

Stress-related illness costs the nation $300 billion a year.

At the Mayo Clinic, 80-88% of patients were ill directly or indirectly because of mental stress. Some 43% of Americans categorize themselves as disorganized and 21% have missed vital work deadlines. Nearly half say disorganization causes them to work late at least two or more times per week, creating more stress. Finally, 48% of employees feel un-loved/un-valued at work. (American Psychological Association) What happened to the American worker?

88% of our medical expenditures are stress-related.

According to the *Wall Street Journal*, office workers waste an average of 40% of their workday because they were never taught organizing skills with which to cope with increasing workloads and demands. Effective time management is a primary means to a less stressful life. A proven Time Investment Plan can help you reduce your stress and reclaim your personal life.

American workers are interrupted seven times an hour.

The average American spends 24 hours a month on social networking sites. During working hours, six out of 10 workers visit social media sites, causing interruptions to the daily working environment. American workers are interrupted seven times an hour at work due to social media. Some 80% of interruptions are trivial and cost the U.S. economy $650 billion each year. (Basex Research)

Interruptions cost the U.S. economy $650 billion a year.

The average person spends nine weeks each year in useless meetings, costing American businesses approximately $37 billion a year. (U.S. Bureau of Labor Statistics)

Useless meetings cost businesses $37 billion a year.

According to the U.S. Small Business Administration, more than 50% of start-up businesses fail within five years. A main reason is lack of planning. People who follow their heart's desire are the most successful. When you follow your heart's desire, it is not a matter of whether you will have it; it is only a matter of time. Never settle for less, and never give up on your heart's desire.

80% of start-up businesses fail within five years.

Small-business owners spend an average of $10,000 to start their businesses, according to a recent Wells Fargo/Gallup Small Business Index. Banks are in the business of making a return on their investment. You need a solid business plan, a proven track record of success and verifiable financial stability before they will even consider loaning money for a new venture. No one will invest in your business unless you are able to pay for it.

The Average American invests $10,000 to start a business.

True success and/or prosperity occurs over time by setting attainable goals, developing a solid plan, setting the appropriate priorities, and investing time, energy and/or money in the areas that will determine your success in life. The Average American wastes a large portion of time chasing get-rich-quick schemes. We are always looking for the easy way. There are no shortcuts to success or prosperity—that's why only a small percentage of people attain it. Everyone gets 24 hours in a day. Success is determined or obtained by how you choose to invest your time. Don't give your time away or let others take your time.

There are no get-rich-quick schemes.

Every night before you go to bed invest 10-15 minutes to think about and identify your Top 5 items or tasks needed to complete the following day for God, Self, Home/Family and Work/Business. Write down the Top 5 items in each category that come to mind and number them according to priority. If you are looking for your American Dream or just to make more money, you need to learn how to invest your time in these four major investment areas. Continue this process for the next seven days.

Every morning when you get up, start working on your number 1 priorities in each of the four major categories. When you have completed the first priorities in each category, start working on priority 2 items in each category until you have complete all your tasks in each category. Continue in this manner until all items on the Top 5 list are complete. Continue this process for seven days.

Additionally, you may have several other areas of interest that require a time investment. Write down any other projects you might be involved with that will require a time investment, such as church, a basketball team, PTA, etc.

Here's an example of how you can list the Top 5 of the four "walls" (major categories).

TIME INVESTMENT PLAN

TIP #5
It's Your Time
Learn how to balance
your time.

Top 5 Model Expanded

	Top 5
Priority	**God**
4	Meditation
5	Reflection
2	Daily Word
3	Read Bible
1	Pray
Priority	**Self**
4	Read book
5	Haircut
2	Take vitamins
3	No sweets
1	Exercise
Priority	**Family/Home**
4	File taxes
5	School play
2	Pick up kids
3	Budget/bills
1	Cut grass
Priority	**Work/Business**
4	Call customer
5	Conference call
3	Marketing meeting
2	Complete presentation
1	Read contract
Priority	**Church**
4	Contact secretary
5	Pick up package
2	Prepare lesson
3	Youth fundraiser
1	Pay tithes

NOTES

PRINCIPLE #6
BUDGET YOUR TIME

At this point, you have been using the Top 5 model along with prioritization to balance your time investments in the four major areas for the past seven days. If you have kept up with the program, you have already invested 28 days learning how to invest your time. It typically takes 21 days to develop a habit, and you have been investing your time for the past 20 days. Congratulations to you if you have followed this program and developed the habit of investing your time!

Congratulations on learning how to invest your time!

Over the final two days of the 30-day process, you will learn how to apply what you have learned about investing your time to a form that will help you budget and plan your day to help maximize your success. The Daily Clean Sheet™ form is used every night to help you plan, budget and organize your time investments, assuming you get another 24 hours.

Daily Clean Sheet™ is used to budget and organize your time.

The Daily Clean Sheet™ form has three main sections. The first section, on the left, is the standard Top 5 format you have been using for the past 28 days. You should be very familiar with this section. Use this section to list your Top 5 items in each of the four major categories. The second section, in the middle, provides a time scale ranging from 6am–12 midnight. This is the typical period of operation and activity for the Average American. Utilize this section to budget time for planned, scheduled or confirmed meetings or events. This section should be filled in before you begin assigning a time budget for additional tasks. The third section of the form can used to write down new action items that come up during the day or to plan additional categories.

Here is a diagram of the Daily Clean Sheet™ form.

DAILY CLEAN SHEET™ FORM (Example 1)

Priority	Date	Time	Budgeted My Time	New Action Items
	GOD			
		6 am		
		7 am		
		8 am		
	SELF			
		9 am		
		10 am		
		11 am		
	HOME/FAMILY			
		Noon		
		1 pm		
		2 pm		
	WORK/SCHOOL			
		3 pm		
		4 pm		
	.	5pm		
	CHURCH			
		6 pm		
		7pm		
		8 pm		
		9 pm		
		10 pm		
		11 pm		
		midnight		

DAILY CLEAN SHEET™ FORM (Complete)

Priority	Date	Time	Budgeted My Time	New Action Items
	GOD			1 Call plumber
1	Pray/read6am	6 am	GOD TIME	2 Plan men breakfast
3	Read Sunday school lesson			3 Appointment with doctor
2	Daily meditation	7 am		4
			SELF TIME	5
		8 am		
	SELF		WORK TIME	6
1	Exercise	9 am		7
3	Read book		Conference call	8
2	Organize	10 am		9
			WORK TIME	10
		11 am		11
	HOME/FAMILY			12
3	Plan vacation budget	Noon	Business lunch/customer	13
1	Review family budget			14
4	Kids shopping	1 pm		15
2	House cleaning			16
		2 pm	Product presentation	
	WORK/SCHOOL			17
2	Review project plan	3 pm		
1	Book travel to Dallas		WORK TIME	
3	Complete presentation	4 pm		
4	Schedule engineering mtg.	5pm		
			HOME TIME	
	CHURCH	6 pm	Dinner	
1	Prepare lesson			
2	Confirm NEM golf course	7pm	FAMILY TIME	
3	Contact sponsors			
		8 pm		
			SELF TIME	
		9 pm		
		10 pm	BED TIME	
		11 pm		
		midnight		

Daily Clean Sheet™ has three main sections.

Every night before you go to bed, use the Daily Clean Sheet™ form to write down your Top 5 list along with the priority. In the middle section, budget time for the events and meetings you already have confirmed. Next, use the right section to list any new items that might come up during the following day, or utilize this section to add more categories. Next is a diagram highlighting a fully populated Daily Clean Sheet™ form.

The Daily Clean Sheet™ form should be used every night before you go to bed to help you budget and plan your next day. Remember that budgeting your time is not about what you need to do, it's about where you want to go.

Budgeting your time is about getting where you want to go.

The next form we need to discuss is the Weekly Clean Sheet™ form. The Weekly Clean Sheet™ form is used as a seven-day forecast to budget and plan your time for the upcoming week. In the Home/Family section, I recommended having a weekly family meeting to discuss any upcoming events or plans that might require your time.

Weekly Clean Sheet™ is your seven-day time forecast.

Every Sunday evening before you go to bed, invest about 30 minutes of your time to have a meeting with your family. Discuss and determine any items that will require your time. On your Weekly Clean SheetTM form, budget time for any special events, teacher conferences, outings or meetings that will require a time investment in your family. Please see the following form.

WEEKLY CLEAN SHEET™ (Example 1)

DAY														
						WORK WEEKLY PLAN								
TIME	MON	TIME	TUES	TIME	WED	TIME	THURS	TIME	FRI	TIME	SAT	TIME	SUN
6		6		6		6		6		6		6	
7		7		7		7		7		7		7	
8		8		8		8		8		8		8	
9		9		9		9		9		9		9	
10		10		10		10		10		10		10	
11		11		11		11		11		11		11	
12		12		12		12		12		12		12	
1		1		1		1		1		1		1	
2		2		2		2		2		2		2	
3		3		3		3		3		3		3	
4		4		4		4		4		4		4	
5		5		5		5		5		5		5	
6		6		6		6		6		6		6	
7		7		7		7		7		7		7	
8		8		8		8		8		8		8	
9		9		9		9		9		9		9	
10		10		10		10		10		10		10	
11		11		11		11		11		11		11	
12		12		12		12		12		12		12	

Time can't be saved. Use it or lose it.

WEEKLY CLEAN SHEET™ (Example 2)

WORK WEEKLY PLAN													
DAY													
TIME	MON	TIME	TUES	TIME	WED	TIME	THURS	TIME	FRI	TIME	SAT	TIME	SUN
6	Pray & Read Bed/Wash	6		6	Pray & Read Bed/Wash	6	Health Club	6	Pray & Read Bed/Wash	6		6	
7	Dress/Eat	7	Health Club	7	Dress/Eat	7		7	Dress/Eat	7	Breakfast	7	
8		8	Conference Call	8	CUSTOMER MEET	8	Kids School	8		8		8	
9		9		9		9	Health Club	9	WORK	9		9	Church
10	WORK	10	WORK	10	WORK	10		10		10		10	
11		11		11		11		11		11		11	
12	Lunch	12	Lunch	12	Lunch	12	Lunch	12	Lunch	12	Lunch	12	
1		1		1		1		1		1	GAME	1	
2		2		2		2		2		2		2	
3	WORK	3	WORK	3	WORK	3	OFF SITE MEETING	3	WORK	3		3	Church Anniversary
4		4		4		4		4		4	House Work	4	
5		5		5		5		5		5		5	
6	Dinner	6	Dinner	6		6	HAIR CUT BARBER	6	Health Club	6		6	
7	PTA MEETING	7	BASKET-BALL GAME	7	STUDY TIME	7		7		7		7	
8		8		8	HOME-WORK	8	DRIVE TEST	8	Dinner	8	Baby-sitting Date	8	WEEKLY PLAN
9	Bed time	9	Bed time	9		9		9		9		9	Bed time
10		10		10	School Prep Bed time	10	School Prep Bed time	10	Free Time/TV	10		10	
11		11		11		11		11	Bed time	11		11	
12		12		12		12		12		12		12	

The Weekly Clean Sheet™ Example 1 is used every week to help you plan your time. I invest 30 minutes of my time every Sunday afternoon during the family meeting to plan how to invest my time for the upcoming week. Time can't be saved. Use it or lose it.

Time can't be saved. Use it or lose it.

The Weekly Clean Sheet™ Example 2 is an example of a completed form. Use this form every week to help you plan your time. I typically invest 30 minutes of my time every Sunday afternoon during the family meeting to plan how to invest my time for the upcoming week.

TIME INVESTMENT PLAN

TIP #6
It's Your Time
Learn how to budget
your time.

PRINCIPLE #7
ESTABLISH YOUR TIME

Establishing your time by setting goals is the final principle for the success of your Time Investment Plan. So many people have high aspirations about becoming rich, or they dream about accomplishing some great goal or task in order to fulfill their lifelong purpose. To invest your time and maximize your success in life, you must first establish a goal. Establishing a goal is not an event, it's a destination.

Establish your goal as your destination.

Establishing your goal tells your mind, "Here's where I want to go." Once you have established a specific goal or task, you will need to verify if it's achievable or just a fantasy. To determine if you can achieve the goal or task, ask yourself the following questions.

1. **Is this goal specific?** Your goal must be something specific. Many people say they want to be rich, but you need a specific goal so you can know when you have achieved it. For example, instead of being vague about being rich, establish a specific goal of $10,000 a month in income.

2. **Is this goal achievable?** Your goal must be achievable. You must have an opportunity or venue that provides you the possibility to achieve your goal. You can't just say, "This is what I want," with no way of achieving it. You have to be able to see yourself achieving the dream. Being able to see a way to

accomplish your dream gives validity to your goal. For example, you goal could be to write a book about time investments.

3. **What's your timeframe to accomplish the goal?** Your goal must have a specific target or deadline. By setting a deadline (for example, two years), you are activating the goal-setting process.

4. **Is this goal realistic?** Analyze your goal to determine if you are being too optimistic. Ask a friend, mentor or accountability partner if this goal is realistic or if it needs to be re-evaluated.

Most people have short-term and long-term goals, but this process will work for both. A short-term goal or task can consist of something to complete in a day, week, month or year. A long-term goal can span several years.

Most people have short- and long-term goals.

Once you establish and verify your goal and assign a specific date, you might need to break your goal into manageable sub-goals that can be accomplished on a monthly, weekly and/or daily basis. Many people are intimidated by goal-setting because it can be overwhelming, but if you follow this simple Time Investment Plan, you will be able to maximize your time and achieve your goals.

Break your goal into smaller, manageable sub-goals.

Breaking your goal into sub-goals allows you to focus on accomplishing your goals in smaller portions, which can give you a greater sense of accomplishment and reduces the possibility of becoming overwhelmed. For example, if you have a goal to write a

300-page book in a year, you can break it into sub-goals of 25 pages a month, or 6.25 pages a week or approximately one page a day. Setting a goal to write one page a day is much more manageable then setting a goal to write a 300-page book in a year.

Brainstorming reveals the action steps to your dream.

Once you have identified, acknowledged, verified and written down your goal, invest time to brainstorm or think about what action items you must complete to accomplish your goals or make your dreams come true. Brainstorming is the creative process of thinking or generating ideas. The brainstorming process can last from 10 minutes up to several hours, depending on your specific goal. Brainstorming is the most magical part of goal-setting because you get the opportunity to see what it takes to make your dream come true.

Brainstorming is the most magical part of goal-setting.

Once you complete the brainstorming process, I recommend creating a picture or visual of your dream or goal. For example, if your dream is to take your family on a Disney cruise vacation, locate a picture of a cruise ship and post it on your mirror, door or dream board to remind you every day of your goal until you do whatever it takes to accomplish it.

Review your goals every year.

Every year, review your past goals, objectives, accomplishments and milestones. Keep a yearly calendar with all the major accomplishments, goals and dates. Every year we invest the time to review the calendar and verify our time-investment portfolio.

Use the Clean Sheet™ Yearly form to write down yearly goals.

After reviewing your past goals, your next step in the Time Investment Plan is to invest time to re-establish new goals based on your objectives and expectations. The Time Investment Plan Clean Sheet™ Yearly model can be used to write down specific and realistic goals in the four major categories of God, Self, Home/Family and Work/Business. Next, prioritize each goal per category in the order of importance. For an effective planning process, always set realistic deadline dates for each goal or task.

Always set realistic goals and dates for each goal.

The high priority items should always be completed first. Also, quarterly meetings should be held to review and re-establish any new goals. Once you establish your yearly goals, you will need to break each goal into smaller monthly, weekly and daily objectives required to accomplish the tasks.

The majority of people are looking to either accomplish a major goal or overcome a major problem in their life. The key to accomplishing your goals is to focus on them day by day. Somebody once said, "How do you eat an elephant? The same way you eat everything else, bite by bite." We can't focus on completing the entire goal at one time, but we can focus on completing our task for today. You can also utilize the Daily Clean Sheet™ and Weekly Clean Sheet™ forms to help you plan your time.

CLEAN SHEET™ YEARLY GOALS

Priority	Goals	Date	Target
	GOD		
1	Read entire Bible	8:30am	3 chapters per day
2	Pray three times per day	6am, 12noon, 6pm	15 minutes per session
3	Read daily devotion	8:45am	15 minutes per session
4	Fast once per week	1st Wednesday	Once per month
	SELF		
1	Exercise daily	1 hour	1 hour per day (6 days)
2	Read book	2 weeks	2 per month
	HOME		
1	Increase income	June	25% increase YOY
2	Plan vacation budget	December	Disney cruise – Fantasy
3	Family car	July	Car for kids in July
	WORK/BUSINESS		
1	Number #1 Sales	January	25% above monthly sales quota
2	Subject matter expert	3 months	Study products 3 hours/night
	CHURCH		
1	Minister training program	October	Minister license – complete
2	Join new group		Men Ministry

The key is to focus on your goals day by day.

We can only invest time in today, so why worry today about tomorrow when you haven't invested all your time in today?

At the beginning of each month, invest time to write in your calendar all of the important dates. Write down birthdays, visitation dates, training classes, entertainment events, holidays and any other events where you might need to budget your time.

CLEAN SHEET™ YEARLY GOALS (Example 3)

Priority	Goals	Date	Target
	GOD		
1			
2			
3			
4			
	SELF		
1			
2			
	HOME		
2			
1			
3			
	WORK/BUSINESS		
1			
2			
	CHURCH		
1			
2			

TIME INVESTMENT PLAN

TIP #7

It's Your Time
Learn how to establish
your time.

NOTES

AFTERWORD

Success in life is determined by the effective use of one's time. Time is your most valuable resource in life. Time is like money—to maximize your success in life, it needs to be invested in the appropriate areas. You ultimately become whatever you invest your time in. Everyone and everything in life is competing to get your time. Your time is your life. If they get your time, they get your mind. If they get your mind, they get your money. If they get your money, they get your life. Establishing the right priorities is the key to investing your time.

Success in life is determined by the effective use of one's time.

Americans must learn to dream again. We all have the same amount of time per day, but we are all unique in our personal design. We must all consciously study our unique talents, abilities, gifts and skills and identify areas in the marketplace that create financial opportunities to utilize our strengths and maximize our life.

Americans must invest time to dream again.

You should invest time to discover what you were you born to be, not what you are trying to do. Life is a journey, not a task. Find out where you are going. Some people find their purpose early in life, but most people discover their purpose along life's journey. Sometimes awareness comes in the form of a dream, or from someone recognizing a particular quality or ability that's above average. No matter how it comes, we all need to be seeking in order to discover our hidden talents, abilities, gifts and skills.

What if you have already discovered your purpose and accomplished your dream? I recommend a line from one of the classic movies of all time, *The Adventures of Sharkboy and Lavagirl:* "Dream a better dream." That's it! When you accomplish one dream, keep dreaming. That, too, is the American Dream.

Dream another dream.

One of the characters in the movie *Lion King* says, "Yesterday is history, tomorrow is a mystery, but today is a gift. That's why they call it the present."

It's Your Time; today is the only time to live your dream. The only time we can live in is today. Yesterday time is gone, and tomorrow time might not come, but if you are alive, invest your time in today! *It's Your Time*; today is the only time to live your dream.

Today is the only time you can live your dream.

The benchmark for obtaining financial success used to be an income of $100,000 a year. Due to increases in the cost of living, the bad economy and rising inflation, the new benchmark is an income of $250,000 a year. This group is defined as the "upper class" and consists of the top 1% of Americans.

Families with household incomes exceeding $75,000 are considered affluent. Families with a net worth of $1 million or more are considered rich. Your success is based upon how much time you are willing to invest.

You only get 24 hours of time per day. There are four things you can do with your time: waste it, spend it, lose it or invest it. Wasted time adds no value to your life. Time merely spent does not yield a return, and lost time can never be found. Time invested in the right areas yields the highest return on your investment goal. Time is your life. The way you invest your minutes, hours and days will determine your success in life. Stop being an Average American!

"IT'S YOUR TIME"

TO LIVE YOUR AMERICAN DREAM

NOTES

THE FOLLOWING THREE
FORMS ARE FOR YOUR USE IN
MANAGING YOUR TIME

DAILY CLEAN SHEET™ FORM

Priority	Date	Time	Budgeted My Time	New Action Items
		6 am		
		7 am		
		8 am		
		9 am		
		10 am		
		11 am		
		Noon		
		1 pm		
		2 pm		
		3 pm		
		4 pm		
	.	5pm		
		6 pm		
		7pm		
		8 pm		
		9 pm		
		10 pm		
		11 pm		
		Midnight		

WEEKLY CLEAN SHEET™

WORK WEEKLY PLAN													
DAY													
TIME	MON	TIME	TUES	TIME	WED	TIME	THURS	TIME	FRI	TIME	SAT	TIME	SUN
6		6		6		6		6		6		6	
7		7		7		7		7		7		7	
8		8		8		8		8		8		8	
9		9		9		9		9		9		9	
10		10		10		10		10		10		10	
11		11		11		11		11		11		11	
12		12		12		12		12		12		12	
1		1		1		1		1		1		1	
2		2		2		2		2		2		2	
3		3		3		3		3		3		3	
4		4		4		4		4		4		4	
5		5		5		5		5		5		5	
6		6		6		6		6		6		6	
7		7		7		7		7		7		7	
8		8		8		8		8		8		8	
9		9		9		9		9		9		9	
10		10		10		10		10		10		10	
11		11		11		11		11		11		11	
12		12		12		12		12		12		12	

CLEAN SHEET™ YEARLY GOALS FORM

Priority	Goals	Date	Target
	GOD		
1			
2			
3			
4			
	SELF		
1			
2			
	HOME		
2			
1			
3			
	WORK/BUSINESS		
1			
2			
	CHURCH		
1			
2			

NOTES

NOTES